Stories
for reading
comprehension 1

L A Hill

Longman ▦

INTRODUCTION

This is the first of a series of three books which have been written to replace my *Comprehension and Précis Pieces*, and *Further Comprehension and Précis Pieces* written with R. D. S. Fielden.

In this series of reading comprehension passages, the vocabulary and structures are carefully graded. The grading follows that of the *Longman Structural Readers*. Book 1 of this series covers Stages 1 and 2 of those readers; Book 2 covers Stages 2 and 3; and Book 3, Stages 4 and 5. Words outside the grading are given at the end of each book.

In this series, the comprehension questions contain no composition element; the students simply have to choose between alternatives which are supplied to them.

The series also contains grammatical exercises. The instructions for these sometimes contain words which are outside the grading. They are therefore more suitable for class than private use, unless the student has someone who can explain the difficult words. In a class, the teacher should explain such difficult words to the students before asking them to do an exercise. In nearly all the grammatical exercises, the student has to choose between alternatives which he or she is given.

L. A. Hill

1

Mr Jones's shop sold food. Mr Jones and a young man worked there. The young man's name was George.

A man came into the shop on Monday. He was a funny man. Mr Jones was in the office. It was behind the shop. The funny man looked at George and said, "I want a small table, please."

George said, "We don't sell tables in this shop. We sell food."

The man smiled and answered, "A small, brown table." He took a picture out of his bag and showed it to George. It was a picture of a small, brown table.

George put his mouth near the man's ear and said, "We do not have tables in this shop! Food! Not tables!"

The man smiled and answered, "That's good. Thank you." Then he sat down on a chair and waited.

George was not happy. He went into the office and spoke to Mr Jones. Then he and Mr Jones came out again.

Mr Jones was angry. He looked at the man and said, "What do you want?"

The man smiled and answered, "I want a loaf of brown bread, please. Haven't you got any bread in your shop?"

Mr Jones said, "Yes, we have." He looked at George, and then he went and got a loaf of brown bread from a big box and gave it to the man.

3

Exercise 1

Look at these questions. Find the right answers. Then write the questions and the answers:

1 Did Mr Jones work in George's shop?
  a) No, he didn't. b) Yes, he did.
2 Who worked in Mr Jones's shop?
  a) A funny man did. b) George did.
3 Did the shop sell tables, or food?
  a) It sold food. b) It sold tables.
4 Did the funny man ask George for some food?
  a) No, he didn't. b) Yes, he did.
5 Did the funny man ask George for a table?
  a) No, he didn't. b) Yes, he did.
6 Did George show him a table?
  a) No, he didn't. b) Yes, he did.
7 Whose office did George go into then?
  a) Mr Jones's. b) The funny man's.
8 Did Mr Jones speak to the funny man?
  a) No, he didn't. b) Yes, he did.
9 Was Mr Jones happy, or angry?
  a) He was angry. b) He was happy.
10 Did the funny man ask Mr Jones for a table, or some food?
  a) A table. b) Some food.

Exercise 2

Write this story. Choose the right words each time:

Mr Jones sold (*food/tables and chairs*) in his shop. His shop was (*behind/in front of*) his office. A (*funny/young*) man worked in the shop too. (*A/The*) funny man came into the shop on Monday. He asked (*George/Mr Jones*) for a (*chair/table*). Then he showed George a (*picture of a table/table*). George (*did not sell/sold*) the funny man a small, brown table. The funny man (*smiled/was not happy*). He sat down and (*waited/was angry*). Then (*George/the funny man*) brought Mr Jones out of the (*office/shop*). Mr Jones (*smiled/was not happy*). The funny man asked him for a (*loaf of brown bread/small, brown table*), and Mr Jones gave (*him a big box/it to him*).

Exercise 3

> Use *a/an* when we can count a thing, and *some* when we cannot. Use *an* only when the next word begins with *a*, *e*, *i*, *o*, or *u*, or an *h* which is not pronounced (e.g. *an hour*).

Look at these pictures. Put *a*, *an*, or *some*, in the empty places:

  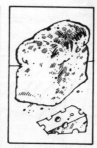 

1 George is eating . . . meal. He is putting . . . food in his mouth with . . . fork.

2 Now George is putting . . . butter on his bread with . . . knife.

3 This is . . . loaf of bread. There is . . . cheese near it.

4 This is . . . egg. It is in . . . water.

5 This is . . . glass. There is . . . milk in it.

6 There is . . . tea in this cup. There is . . . spoon in it.

7 This is . . . cup too. There is . . . coffee in it.

8 This is . . . picture of . . . table.

Gladys was at school in a small, quiet town in England. She was sixteen years old, and her father and mother were poor, and their house was very small.

Maisie was Gladys's friend. She went to that school as well. Gladys said, "Maisie, I'm going to find a very rich man and I'm going to marry him. Then I'm going to have a beautiful house and a large garden, and a lot of clothes, and a lot of money."

Maisie smiled and said, "Where are you going to find a very rich man, Gladys? There aren't any in our town."

But Gladys was a very pretty girl. Her eyes were blue, and her hair was black and soft. She went to London, and then she went to America. She found a tall, very rich man there, and she married him. She was twenty-two years old then.

Then she and her husband went to England. They went to Gladys's old house, and Maisie came there.

Gladys said, "I've married a very rich man, Maisie, and I've got a beautiful house and a large garden and four gardeners. And I've bought a lot of clothes and I have money as well. My husband's got a plane too, and he flies it!"

Maisie said, "A lot of people have got planes and fly them, Gladys."

"In their house?" Gladys asked.

Exercise 1

Look at these questions. Find the right answers. Then write the questions and the answers:

1 Were Gladys's father and mother rich?
   a) No, they were not.   b) Yes, they were.
2 Did Gladys want to work in her small, quiet town?
   a) No, she did not.   b) Yes, she did.
3 Who did Gladys want to marry?
   a) A rich man.   b) A tall man.
4 Were there any very rich men in Gladys's town?
   a) No, there were not.   b) Yes, there were a lot.   c) Yes, there were some.
5 Did Gladys marry in London, or in America?
   a) In London.   b) In America.
6 Was her husband a short man?
   a) No, he was tall.   b) Yes, he was.
7 Where did Maisie see Gladys again?
   a) In America.   b) In London.   c) In their small town.
8 Whose house did they meet in?
   a) Gladys's old house.   b) Maisie's house.
9 Who flew the plane in this story?
   a) Gladys did.   b) Gladys's husband did.
10 Where did he or she fly it?
   a) In the garden.   b) In the house.

Exercise 2

Write this story. Choose the right words each time:

Gladys's school was in a (*city/town/village*), (*and/but*) Maisie's was in a (*city/town/village*). Gladys lived in a (*big/small*) house. She had (*black/blue*) eyes, (*and/but*) she was (*beautiful/not beautiful*). She went to America (*after/before*) she went to London. She married a man in (*America/London*). Then she went back to England (*with/without*) her husband. She met Maisie there. (*Gladys/Maisie*) had a very rich husband now. He had (*a plane/two planes*). (*A lot of people/He*) flew (*it/them*) in their house.

Exercise 3

We use the *have/has done* tense—the present perfect (e.g. *has been*, *have opened*) when the result of the action is still there; but we use the *did* tense — the past simple (e.g. *saw*, *opened*) when it is not, or when the time at which it happened is given.

Look at these examples:

Gladys has opened the window. Look! It is open.

Gladys opened the window at 2 o'clock, but now she has shut it. Look! It is shut.

Put *bought*, *has bought*, *came*, *has come*, *went*, *has gone*, *married*, *has married*, *sold* or *has sold*, in the empty places:

1 Gladys isn't here now. She . . . to America.

2 This is America. Gladys . . . here in 1981, and now she . . . a tall, rich man.

3 Gladys . . . to America in 1981, but now she . . . back to England. She is saying, "This is Tom. We . . . in America in 1982."

4 Tom . . . this car from a man in January, but now he . . . it to a lady. It isn't his now.

3

Alan Smith's father bought him a small shop, and Alan sold milk, butter, cheese, eggs and other things in it. His shop was in a small town, and it was open on Tuesday, Wednesday, Thursday, Friday and Saturday, and on Sunday morning, but it was shut on Sunday afternoon and on Monday.

Alan went to some farms on Monday and bought their best butter and cheese and eggs from the farmers, but he bought his milk in the town. A truck brought it to his shop in the morning. Alan and his wife worked in the shop, and they sold a lot of their food, because it was good and clean.

A fat woman came into the shop on Saturday. She bought some eggs and some butter, and then she said to Alan's wife, "Your eggs and your butter are dear today. Why are Saturday and Sunday dearer than Tuesday, Wednesday, Thursday and Friday?"

Alan's wife was unhappy. She looked at the fat woman, and then she looked at Alan, but she did not give an answer. Then Alan smiled and said, "Our food is not dearer on Saturday and Sunday! It is cheaper on Tuesday, Wednesday, Thursday and Friday!"

Exercise 1

Look at these questions. Find the right answers. Then write the questions and the answers:

1   Was Alan's shop open on Monday?
    a) No, it wasn't.   b) Yes, it was.

2   Was Alan's shop shut on Saturday?
    a) No, it wasn't.   b) Yes, it was.

3   Was Alan's shop open or shut on Sunday morning?
    a) It was open.   b) It was shut.

4   Who sold Alan cheese?
    a) His father did.   b) The farmers did.

5   Who brought Alan's butter to his shop?
    a) A man in a truck did.   b) Alan did.

6   Who brought milk to Alan's shop?
    a) A man in a truck did.   b) Alan did.

7   Why did a lot of people buy food from Alan?
    a) Because he and his wife worked in the shop.
    b) Because the food was clean and good.

8   Who answered the fat woman's question?
    a) Alan did.   b) Alan's wife did.

9   Was the answer an angry one, or a nice one?
    a) It was a nice one.   b) It was an angry one.

10 Was the food in the shop dearer on Friday or on Saturday?
    a) It was dearer on Friday.   b) It was dearer on Saturday.

Exercise 2

Write this story. Choose the right words each time:

(*Alan/Alan's father*) bought a shop for (*him/his father*). He (*did not sell any/sold*) food in it, and it was open (*every day/5½ days*) of the week. Alan (*bought/sold*) things on Monday. The farmers (*bought/sold*) him food (*and/but not*) milk on their farms. (*He brought them/They sold him*) the best butter and cheese and eggs.

The (*food/milk*) came to Alan's shop in a truck. Alan's wife (*did not work/worked*) with him. (*Alan and his wife were/Alan's food was*) good and clean. A fat woman came into the shop. Alan's wife was unhappy because she (*asked a question/was fat*). (*Alan's wife/Alan*) answered the question. The food in the shop was (*cheaper/dearer*) on Saturday and Sunday.

Exercise 3

> Use *any* in questions (e.g. "Have you got any butter?") and in negative statements (e.g. "We haven't got any butter."), but use *some* when there is no question and no negative (e.g. "We have got some butter.").

Put *some* or *any* in the empty places:

1 "Have you got . . . hard cheese?"
"No, we haven't got . . . hard cheese, but we have got . . . nice soft cheese."

2 "I want . . . eggs. Have you got . . . brown ones?"
"Yes, we have got . . . nice brown ones."

3 "You haven't got . . . fruit."
"No, we don't have . . . fruit here, but there are . . . oranges and apples in that shop."

4 "Have you got . . . milk?"
"We haven't got . . . milk now, but we're going to have . . . bottles this afternoon."

11

4

Mr and Mrs Brown had two daughters and two sons. Both the daughters married, and then both the sons married too. Soon Mr and Mrs Brown had a granddaughter, and then they had two grandsons. They were very happy.

Then one of their daughters had another baby, and she telephoned her mother, "Please come and help with your new granddaughter." Mrs Brown went quickly, but Mr Brown stayed at home, because he was nearer his job there. But he said, "I'll come on Friday evening, and I'll stay till Monday morning."

On Friday evening, after work, Mr Brown got into a train. He was very happy. "I'm going to see my new granddaughter now," he said.

There were three empty places in the train. There was an old man beside one empty place, and Mr Brown went to him and said nicely, "Are you a grandfather?"

"Yes," the man answered, "I have three granddaughters."

Mr Brown went to the second empty place. There was a nice woman beside that. Mr Brown said to her, "Are you a grandmother?"

The woman answered, "Yes, I have two granddaughters and two grandsons."

Mr Brown went to the third empty place. There was a man beside that, and Mr Brown said to him, "And are you a grandfather?"

"No, I'm not," the man answered.

Mr Brown smiled happily and said, "That's good." He sat down in the empty place and said to the man kindly, "Now I'll tell you about my granddaughters and grandsons."

Exercise 1

Look at these questions. Find the right answers. Then write the questions and the answers:

1 Did Mr and Mrs Brown have any children?
a) Yes, they had four.   b) Yes, they had two.

2 Did their children marry?
a) No, they did not.   b) Yes, all of them did.   c) Yes, two of them did.

3 How many granddaughters did Mr and Mrs Brown have?
a) One.   b) Two.

4 Did they have any grandsons?
a) No, they did not.   b) Yes, they had two.

5 Who went and helped their daughter with her new baby?
a) Mr Brown did.   b) Mrs Brown did.

6 Did Mr Brown go with his wife?
a) No, he did not.   b) Yes, he did.

7 Why?
a) Because he was ill.
b) Because he had a job near his home.

8 When did Mr Brown go to his daughter's house?
a) On Friday evening.   b) On Monday morning.

9 How did he go?
a) In a train.   b) In his car.

10 What did he do all the time in the train?
a) He talked about his granddaughters and grandsons.
b) He listened to stories about other people's grand-daughters and grandsons.

Exercise 2

Write this story. Choose the right words each time:

Mr and Mrs Brown (*did not have any/had two*) daughters, (*and/but*) they (*did not have any/had two*) sons. Mr and Mrs Brown's children (*did not have any/had some*) children too. Mrs

Brown (*did not help/helped*) one of her (*daughters/sons*) with (*her/his*) new baby. She went to her (*daughter's/son's*) house (*with/without*) her husband, because his job was (*near/not near*) the (*daughter's/son's*) house. Mr Brown (*did not work/worked*) on Saturday and Sunday, so he (*did not go/went*) to stay with his (*daughter/son*) then. He went in a train, and (*did not sit/sat*) beside another (*grandfather/grandmother*), because he only wanted to talk about (*her/his*) granddaughters and grandsons.

Exercise 3

> To change an adjective into an adverb, we usually add *ly* (e.g. *slow, slowly*).

Choose the right word each time:

1 This is a (*slow/slowly*) train. It goes very (*slow/slowly*).

2 Mr Brown is (*happily/happy*). He is smiling (*happily/happy*).

3 The baby is (*hungrily/hungry*). It is eating (*hungrily/hungry*).

4 Mrs Brown and her daughter must be (*quiet/quietly*). They are talking (*quiet/quietly*).

5

Joe was the son of a farmer. His father's farm was poor, and Joe worked on it for a long time, but then his father died, and Joe said, "I needn't stay here now. I'll sell this farm and buy one in a better place. Then I'll soon be rich."

He bought a farm in the east of the country, but then his new neighbours said to him, "The weather's often very bad here. The wind's very strong, and it breaks windows and doors. You must build a room under the ground, and then you and your family can go down there, and you'll be safe from the wind."

So Joe built a room under the ground. It was a lot of work, because the ground was hard.

But after that, the weather was good for a very long time. There was no wind, and Joe spoke angrily. He said, "Why did I listen to my neighbours? I didn't have to make that room under the ground. The wind never blows strongly here."

But then one day there was a very strong wind, and Joe and his family had to go down into their room under the ground. They were there for a long time. Then the wind stopped, and they came up. All the windows and doors in their house were broken.

Joe was not angry about his work now. He smiled happily and said, "Ah! I'm glad I built that room!"

Exercise 1

Look at these questions. Find the right answers. Then write the questions and the answers:

1 What was Joe's father?
   a) He was a farmer.   b) He was a teacher.

2 Was his father rich?
   a) No, he was not.   b) Yes, he was.

3 Why did Joe leave his father's farm?
   a) Because the wind was very strong there.   b) Because he wanted a farm in a better place.

4 Why did he need a room under the ground?
   a) Because the doors and windows of his farm were broken.   b) Because there were very strong winds in that place.

5 Did the wind often blow strongly after that?
   a) No, it did not.   b) Yes, it did.

6 Was Joe happy about that?
   a) No, he was not.   b) Yes, he was.

7 Why did he go down into the room under the ground one day?
   a) Because the weather was very cold.   b) Because there was a very strong wind.

8 Who went with him?
   a) His family did.   b) His new neighbours did.

9 What did the wind do?
   a) It broke the windows and doors of Joe's house.   b) It went down into the room under the ground.

10 Was Joe sad then?
   a) No, he was happy.   b) Yes, he was.

Exercise 2

Write this story. Choose the right words each time:

Joe worked on his (*father's/son's*) farm. It was a (*poor/rich*) farm, because it was in a (*bad/good*) place. Then Joe bought (*another/the*) farm, and he (*bought/made*) a room under the ground, because his (*father/neighbours*) said, "The (*weather/wind*) can (*be/blow*) very (*good/strongly*) here, and you will not be safe in your house then." But the (*weather was/wind did*) not (*blow/good*) for a long time, and Joe was (*angry/happy*), because he (*did not need/needed*) his room under the ground. Then (*the wind stopped/there was a very strong wind*), and it broke the doors and windows of Joe's (*house/room under the ground*). He was (*happy/sad*) after that.

Exercise 3

> *Must* shows obligation (e.g. "The wind is very strong, so Joe and his family must go down into the room under the ground.").
>
> If we want to show that there is no obligation, we can use *needn't* (e.g. "Joe and his family needn't stay under the ground now, because the wind has stopped.").
>
> For the past tense of *must*, we can use *had to*, and for the past tense of *needn't*, we can use *didn't need to*.

Put *must, had to, needn't* or *didn't need to* in the empty places:

Joe said, "I want to be rich, so I . . . buy a farm in a better place." He wanted to be rich, so he . . . buy a farm in a better place. Then Joe said, "I've got a lot of cows, so I . . . buy others." Joe had a lot of cows, so he . . . buy others.

Lynn was five years old. She had a lot of little friends. They were older, and they were at school. These children told Lynn nice stories about school, so Lynn wanted to go there too.

Then one day her mother said, "You can go to school now, Lynn," and Lynn was very happy.

She was the youngest child in the school, and on the first day, her mother stayed at school with her. But on the second day, Lynn said to her, "You can go home now, Mummy."

Lynn's mother was happy, but she was sad too, because Lynn did not need her all the time now.

Lynn was very happy at school, and she learnt a lot of things there. Her mother always said, "What have you learnt today, Lynn?" and Lynn told her.

One day, Lynn came back from school and said to her mother, "Miss Richards (she was Lynn's teacher) told us some nice stories today, Mummy. The best was about Ulysses. He fought against the . . . the . . . er . . ."

"The Trojans," her mother said.

"Oh, yes, that's right," Lynn answered. "The Trojans. And then Ulysses went back in his ship with some other men. He went to see his wife . . . er . . . his wife . . ."

"Penelope," Lynn's mother said.

Lynn stopped and looked at her mother. "Mummy," she said, "has someone told you this story already?"

Exercise 1

Look at these questions. Find the right answers. Then write the questions and the answers:

1 Did Lynn have any friends?
   a) No, she did not.   b) Yes, she did.
2 Did they go to school?
   a) No, they did not.   b) Yes, they did.
3 Why did Lynn want to go to school too?
   a) Because her friends told her nice stories about it.
   b) Because her friends were older.
4 Who was the youngest in the school?
   a) Lynn's mother was.   b) Lynn was.
5 Did Lynn's mother stay with her?
   a) No, she didn't.   b) Yes, she stayed with her for one day.   c) Yes, she stayed with her for two days.
6 Was Lynn's mother happy or sad then?
   a) She was happy.   b) She was happy and sad.   c) She was sad.
7 Who was Lynn's teacher?
   a) Lynn's Mummy.   b) Miss Richards.   c) Ulysses.
8 Who fought against the Trojans?
   a) Lynn's Mummy.   b) Miss Richards.   c) Ulysses.
9 Who was Ulysses' wife?
   a) Miss Richards.   b) Penelope.
10 Did Lynn's mother know the story about Ulysses?
   a) No, she did not.   b) Yes, she did.

Exercise 2

Write this story. Choose the right words each time:

Lynn's friends were (happy/not happy) at school, so Lynn (did not want/wanted) to go there too. Then one day her mother (sent/took) her to school. Her mother (stayed there/went home) on the first day, (and/but) she (stayed there/went home) on the second day. She was (happy/sad) because Lynn (did not need/needed) her at school. Lynn (always/never) told her mother about her lessons. One day she told her (a story/some nice stories) about Ulysses. She did not remember (all the/any) names. She forgot

19

the name of (*Penelope's/Ulysses'*) wife, so her mother (*asked/told*) her. The story of Ulysses is a very (*new/old*) one, so her mother (*did not know/knew*) it.

Exercise 3

Most nouns form their plural just by adding *s* (e.g. *friend, friends*). But if a noun ends in a consonant + *y*, the *y* becomes *ies* in the plural (e.g. *story, stories*); and if a noun ends in *fe* the *fe* becomes *ves* (e.g. *wife, wives*).

There are also some irregular plurals (e.g. *child, children; man, men; woman, women*).

This becomes *these* in the plural (e.g. *this girl, these girls*); and *that* becomes *those* (e.g. *that boy, those boys*).

Put the correct letter, or the correct ending, in the empty places:

1 The two teacher... told all the child... some nice stor....

2 Ulysses and some other m...n went home to see their wi....

Put *that*, *those*, *this* or *these* in the empty places:

3 Do you want . . . book?

4 Please bring me . . . books.

5 I like . . . books.

6 Why is . . . book on the floor?

Mr and Mrs Young's small house was in a village, but their children's houses were in a town. Then Mr Young died. Mrs Young was eighty-five years old, and her children said to her, "Come and live in the town near us, Mother. Or come and live in one of our houses." But she said, "No, I'm not going to go to the town. I'm going to remain here."

Her children were not happy. They said, "There are a lot of burglars here now. Maybe one of them will come into her house and take her money and her nice things."

One Sunday one of her daughters went to Mrs Young's house. She saw a key on the ground at the side of the front door. "Mother!" she said, "You mustn't put your key there. That's the worst place. Burglars can see it and open the door!"

Mrs Young smiled. "Try to open the door with the key," she said. Her daughter did this. The key made a lot of noise, but it did not open the door.

Then Mrs Young said, "I hear the key in the lock, and then I get one of my brother's old guns, go out of the back door and creep up behind the burglars."

21

Exercise 1

Look at these questions. Find the right answers. Then write the
questions and the answers:

1 Did Mr and Mrs Young's children live with them?
   a) No, they did not.   b) Yes, they did.

2 Did Mrs Young go and live with her children?
   a) No, she did not.   b) Yes, she did.

3 Why were her children not happy then?
   a) Because a burglar came into their mother's house.
   b) Because there were a lot of burglars in that place.

4 What did one of Mrs Young's daughters see one day?
   a) A key.   b) A lock.

5 Where was it?
   a) In the lock.   b) Near Mrs Young's door.

6 Why is that not a good place for your key?
   a) Because people can see it and open the door with it.
   b) Because you will lose it.

7 Where did Mrs Young's daughter put the key?
   a) In the house.   b) In the lock.

8 Did Mrs Young's daughter open the door with it?
   a) No, she did not.   b) Yes, she did.

9 Why didn't the door open?
   a) Because the key made a lot of noise.   b) Because the
   key was the wrong one.

10 What did Mrs Young always do when she heard the key
    in the lock?
    a) She crept up behind the burglars with a gun.   b) She
    made a lot of noise.

Stories for reading comprehension 1

Answer key

Please unbend staples carefully and detach this key.

KEY

UNIT 1

Exercise 1: 1a, 2b, 3a, 4a, 5b, 6a, 7a, 8b, 9a, 10b
Exercise 2: food, in front of, young, A, George, table, picture of a table, did not sell, smiled, waited, George, office, was not happy, loaf of brown bread, it to him
Exercise 3: 1 a, some, a 2 some, a 3 a, some 4 an, some 5 a, some 6 some, a 7 a, some 8 a, a

UNIT 2

Exercise 1: 1a, 2a, 3a, 4a, 5b, 6a, 7c, 8a, 9b, 10b
Exercise 2: town, and, town, small, blue, and, beautiful, after, America, with, Gladys, a plane, He, it
Exercise 3: 1 has gone 2 came, has married 3 went, has come, married 4 bought, has sold

UNIT 3

Exercise 1: 1a, 2a, 3a, 4b, 5b, 6a, 7b, 8a, 9a, 10b
Exercise 2: Alan's father, him, sold, 5½ days, bought, sold, but not, They sold him, milk, worked, Alan's food was, asked a question, Alan, dearer
Exercise 3: 1 any, any, some 2 some, any, some 3 any, any, some 4 any, any, some

UNIT 4

Exercise 1: 1a, 2b, 3b, 4b, 5b, 6a, 7b, 8a, 9a, 10a
Exercise 2: had two, and, had two, had some, helped, daughters, her, daughter's, without, not near, daughter's, did not work, went, daughter, did not sit, grandfather, his
Exercise 3: 1 slow, slowly, 2 happy, happily 3 hungry, hungrily 4 quiet, quietly

UNIT 5

Exercise 1: 1a, 2a, 3b, 4b, 5a, 6a, 7b, 8a, 9a, 10a
Exercise 2: father's, poor, bad, another, made, neighbours, wind, blow, strongly, wind did, blow, angry, did not need, there was a very strong wind, house, happy
Exercise 3: must, had to, needn't, didn't need to

UNIT 6

Exercise 1: 1b, 2b, 3a, 4b, 5b, 6b, 7b, 8c, 9b, 10b

Exercise 2: happy, wanted, took, stayed there, but, went home, sad, did not need, always, a story, all the, Ulysses', told, old, knew

Exercise 3: 1 teachers, children, stories 2 men, wives 3 this 4 those 5 these 6 that

UNIT 7

Exercise 1: 1a, 2a, 3b, 4a, 5b, 6a, 7b, 8a, 9b, 10a

Exercise 2: stayed in the village, did not live, had some, One of Mrs Young's daughters, her, garden, Mrs Young's daughter, not happy, burglars can open doors with keys, not the right key, made a lot of noise, brother's, crept up behind

Exercise 3: 1 Young's 2 children's 3 sons', daughters'

UNIT 8

Exercise 1: 1b, 2a, 3b, 4b, 5a, 6a, 7b, 8b, 9b, 10c

Exercise 2: went up, he loved it, Sunday, take his fifty pence, money, the seeds, sell, get, go to, be, be, set, Billy, he, the doctor

Exercise 3: She, her, He, her, him, you, I, you, I, we, They, us, I, them

UNIT 9

Exercise 1: 1b, 2b, 3b, 4b, 5a, 6a, 7a, 8a, 9b, 10b

Exercise 2: Europe, Australia, a long time, Hungary, wanted to see, all, Rome, went to Budapest in a train, visited, two, animals, but, did not come, and, came, only understood, lived in Hungary

Exercise 3: all, all, both, Both

UNIT 10

Exercise 1: 1b, 2b, 3a, 4a, 5a, 6b, 7b, 8b, 9a, 10b

Exercise 2: the mountain and hills, rain, full, flood, Red Cross, low land, low, not, the river, went, he, on his roof, came in a boat, took him to higher ground, have any money for them

Exercise 3: 1 much, many 2 much, a lot, much 3 a lot of 4 many, many 5 a lot of, a lot

UNIT **11**

Exercise 1: 1a, 2b, 3b, 4a, 5a, 6a, 7b, 8b, 9b, 10a

Exercise 2: mother, a small bicycle, one, school, his mother's, bicycle, bicycles, do not take, needed, did not have, him, she, him, his, not all, is not

Exercise 3: 1 She, her, It, Its 2 His, He, His, her 3 They, them, Their

UNIT **12**

Exercise 1: 1a, 2b, 3b, 4a, 5b, 6a, 7a, 8a, 9a, 10b

Exercise 2: did not make shoes, but he, villages, there were not many shops, his lorry, door, his window, spoke to, happy, at home, some of his shoes, door, but, did not open, spoke to, right, was, was not

Exercise 3: a, The, some, some, the, a, the, an, some, the, some, a, an

UNIT **13**

Exercise 1: 1b, 2a, 3b, 4b, 5b, 6b, 7a, 8b, 9a, 10b

Exercise 2: England, to New York, did not know, asked for it, plane, a room in, the address, a cinema, in, but he forgot, help him, out, a telegraph office, his

Exercise 3: 1 going 2 coming 3 bringing 4 taking

UNIT **14**

Exercise 1: 1a, 2b, 3b, 4a, 5b, 6b, 7b, 8a, 9a, 10b

Exercise 2: market, but, never, weren't any, before, market, Mary Adams, had, and, wanted, to the bus stop, weren't any, but, got two

Exercise 3: 1 There is, It is 2 There are, They are 3 There is, He is 4 There is, She is

Exercise 2

Write this story. Choose the right words each time:

After her husband died, Mrs Young (*stayed in the village/went and lived in the town*). Her children were not happy then, because she (*did not live/lived*) in one of their houses. Mrs Young (*had some/lost her*) money and nice things. (*One of Mrs Young's daughters/Mrs Young*) visited (*one of her daughters/her*) one Sunday. There was a key in the (*garden/house*) near the front door. (*Mrs Young/Mrs Young's daughter*) saw it and was (*happy/not happy*), because (*burglars can open doors with keys/she wanted to open the door*). But it was (*a very old key/not the right key*), and the door (*opened/made a lot of noise*). Mrs Young had her (*father's/brother's*) old gun, and she (*crept up behind/hit*) the burglars with it.

Exercise 3

To make a singular noun (e.g. *cat*), or a plural noun which does not end in s (e.g. *men*) possessive, put *'s* after it (e.g. *cat* becomes *cat's*, and *men* becomes *men's*); but put *'* after a plural noun which does end in s (e.g. *teachers* becomes *teachers'*).

Put *'s*, *'* or *s'* in the empty places:

1 Mrs Young... house was in a village.

2 Her children... houses were in a town.

3 She had two sons and two daughters. Her son... names were Fred and Bill, and her daughter... names were Jane and Ann.

23

Billy is twelve years old, and his sister is fifteen. It was Saturday yesterday, and Billy's father gave him fifty pence. There is a big tree in Billy's garden, and he climbed it and sat in it. He likes that place in the tree very much.

Then Billy looked at his fifty pence and said, "I'm going to go to the market tomorrow on my bicycle, and I'm going to buy some seeds with this money. Then I'm going to plant them under this tree. I'm going to have a lot of flowers and fruit and plants, and I'm going to sell them.

"A lot of people are going to come to my garden every day, and they're going to buy my nice flowers and fruit and plants, and in the end I'm really going to have a lot of money. Then I'm going to grow up and go to university, and I'm going to be a doctor.

"Then my sister will come to me and say, 'Doctor, Doctor, I've broken my left arm! Please help me!' And I'm going to set her arm."

The sky was blue, the weather was hot, and Billy was tired after that, so he went to sleep in the tree. But then he fell out of the tree and broke his left arm. His mother took him to the doctor, and she set it.

Exercise 1

Look at these questions. Find the right answers. Then write the questions and the answers:

1 Who is older, Billy or his sister?
   a) Billy is.   b) His sister is.

2 Where did Billy sit yesterday?
   a) In a tree.   b) In his house.

3 Where did Billy want to go on Sunday?
   a) To a big tree.   b) To the market.

4 Why did he want to go there?
   a) Because he wanted a bicycle.   b) Because he wanted some seeds.

5 What did he want to do with the seeds?
   a) He wanted to plant them.   b) He wanted to sell them.

6 Why did he want to grow flowers and fruit and plants?
   a) Because he wanted money.   b) Because he wanted to buy them.

7 What did he want to be?
   a) A teacher at a university.   b) A doctor.

8 What did he want to do to his sister then?
   a) He wanted to come to her.   b) He wanted to set her arm.

9 Why did Billy fall out of the tree?
   a) Because he was tired.   b) Because he went to sleep.
   c) Because the weather was hot.

10 Who set his arm?
   a) His mother did.   b) His sister did.   c) The doctor did.

Exercise 2

Write this story. Choose the right words each time:

Billy (*sat under/went up*) a big tree yesterday, because (*he loved it/his father gave it to him*). There was a market on (*Saturday/Sunday*) and Billy wanted to go there. He wanted to (*sell his bicycle/take his fifty pence*) there and buy some seeds with the (*bicycle/money*). Then he wanted to plant (*a tree/the seeds*). He wanted to (*buy/sell*) nice flowers and fruit and plants, and to (*get/give*) a lot of money for them. Then he wanted to (*go to/visit*) the university and to (*be/see*) a doctor. He wanted to (*be/visit*) his sister's doctor, and to (*hold/set*) her arm. But (*Billy/the tree*) fell, and (*he/it*) broke his arm, and (*his mother/his sister/the doctor*) set it.

Exercise 3

Use *he* or *him* when you are writing about a man or a boy, *she/her* when you are writing about a woman or a girl, and *they/them* when you are writing about more than one person. Use *I/me* when the person is speaking about himself/herself, and *you* when the person is addressing someone else. Use *we/us* when the person is speaking about himself or herself plus one or more other people.

Use *he/she/they/I/we* when the word is the subject, and *him/her/them/me/us* when it is the object. *You* can be used both for the subject and for the object.

Put *I*, *you*, *she*, *her*, *he*, *him*, *we*, *us*, *they* or *them* in the empty places:

Ruth is Billy's sister. . . . is fifteen years old. Billy loves . . . very much. . . . said to . . ., "Do you want these flowers, Ruth?" and Ruth said to . . ., "Thank . . ., Billy. . . . don't want flowers now, but . . . can give me some tomorrow. . . . am going to go out with my friend Lily then, and . . . are going to visit some friends. . . . have invited . . . to tea. Lily and . . . can give . . . the flowers then."

In the last fifty years, a lot of people have left Europe and have gone to live in Australia. One of them was a Hungarian man. He lived in Australia for a long time, and after that, he had a lot of good friends. He always said to them, "Australia's beautiful, but Hungary's beautiful too."

Then one year he said, "I'm going to go back to Hungary now to visit my old home." All of his new friends said to him, "We want to go with you, because Hungary's a beautiful country, and we want to see it too."

The Hungarian Australian took all his friends from Sydney to Rome in a big plane, and then they went from Rome to Budapest in a train, because they wanted to see the mountains, and the villages, and the towns.

They stayed in Budapest for four days, and they liked it very much. One day they went to the zoo in Budapest and saw two kangaroos there.

The Australians were very happy, because kangaroos come from Australia. They said to the animals, "Come here, old friends! Come and see your Australian brothers!" But the kangaroos did not move.

But then the Hungarian Australian spoke to the animals in Hungarian. "Come here!" he said, and both the kangaroos ran to him.

The other Australians laughed and said, "Look at that! They're Australian, but they only know Hungarian!"

Exercise 1

Look at these questions. Find the right answers. Then write the questions and the answers:

1 Where is Hungary?
   a) In Australia.   b) In Europe.

2 Did the Hungarian man stay in Australia for a long time?
   a) No, he did not.   b) Yes, he did.

3 Did he have any friends in Australia then?
   a) No, he did not.   b) Yes, he did.

4 Why did he want to go back to Hungary?
   a) Because Australia is beautiful.   b) To visit his old home.

5 Why did his friends want to see Hungary?
   a) Because it is beautiful.   b) To see their old homes.

6 Did they go to Hungary in a ship?
   a) No, they went in a plane, and then in a train.   b) Yes, they did.

7 Where did they find a zoo?
   a) In Budapest.   b) In Rome.

8 What did they see in the zoo?
   a) Some kangaroos.   b) Some old friends.

9 Why didn't the kangaroos come to them?
   a) Because they did not move.   b) Because they did not understand English.

10 Why did the kangaroos only understand Hungarian?
   a) Because they came from Australia.   b) Because they lived in Hungary.

Exercise 2

Write this story. Choose the right words each time:

Hungary is a country in (*Australia/Europe*). The man in this story went from Hungary to (*Australia/Europe*) and stayed there for (*a long time/one year*). Then he wanted to visit his old home in (*Australia/Hungary*). His friends wanted to go too, because they (*came from/wanted to see*) Hungary. So they (*all/both*) flew to (*Rome/Hungary*), and then they (*drove to Budapest/went to Budapest in a train*). They (*stayed in/visited*) the zoo in Budapest. They saw (*a lot of/two*) kangaroos there. The Australians were happy, because kangaroos are Australian (*animals/birds*). They called to the kangaroos in English, (*and/but*) the kangaroos (*came/did not come*). Then the Hungarian man called to them in Hungarian, (*and/but*) they (*came/did not come*). They (*did not understand/only understood*) Hungarian, because they (*lived in Hungary/were Australian*).

Exercise 3

We use *both* when we are talking or writing about two people, animals or things, and *all* when we are talking or writing about more than two.

Put *all* or *both* in the empty places:

The Hungarian man had a lot of friends, and . . . of them went to Budapest with him. There were hundreds of animals in the zoo, and they saw ... the animals. Two of them were kangaroos, and . . . of these kangaroos understood Hungarian, but not English. . . . the kangaroos came to the Hungarian man, but they did not come to the Australians.

10

There was a big flood near our house in spring. The water came down from the mountain and the hills, the river came up and up, and a lot of the houses on the low land were soon under the water.

The Red Cross sent some men, and they brought food and dry clothes, and took some people to higher ground in boats.

One old man lives in a small house near our river. He is a poor man, and there aren't any other houses near his. There was a lot of rain one night, and in the morning the old man looked out of his window and saw the flood. The water was nearly up to his bedroom window.

The water came up and up, and the old man went to the top floor of his house. Then the flood was worse, and he went up on to the roof.

"What am I going to do?" he said. "The water's very deep, and I can't swim."

But after three hours the old man saw a boat. It came slowly near, and the old man saw two young men in it.

"We've come from the Red Cross," one of the young men called, "and . . ."

"I'm sorry," the old man answered, "but I've just given you some money this month, and I haven't got much. I'm a poor man."

Exercise 1

Look at these questions. Find the right answers. Then write the questions and the answers:

1 Where did the flood come from?
   a) A spring.   b) The mountain and hills.

2 Where did the water come up from?
   a) A lot of the houses.   b) The river.

3 Who brought food and dry clothes?
   a) Men from the Red Cross.   b) People on higher ground.

4 Is the poor old man's house near a lot of the houses on the low land?
   a) No, it is not.   b) Yes, it is.

5 When did the old man see the flood?
   a) In the morning.   b) One night.

6 Why did the old man go up on to his roof?
   a) Because he wanted to look for the men from the Red Cross.   b) Because the water was very high.

7 What did the old man do then?
   a) He swam to the higher land.   b) He waited.

8 Who came then?
   a) An old man in a boat.   b) Two young men.

9 Did the young men want money for the Red Cross?
   a) No, they did not.   b) Yes, they did.

10 What did they want?
   a) They wanted to look at the old man.   b) They wanted to take the old man to the high ground.

Exercise 2

Write this story. Choose the right words each time:

Our river comes from (*a lot of the houses on the low land/the mountain and hills*). There was a lot of (*rain/sunshine*) there in spring, so the river was very (*empty/full*), and there was a (*spring/flood*).

Some men came from the (*mountain and hills/Red Cross*) and took people from the (*higher ground/low land*) in boats. One poor man lives on the (*high/low*) ground. His house is (*not/very*) near ours. One night, (*some people/the river*) came nearly up to his bedroom window. The old man (*swam/went*) up to the top of his house. In the end (*he/the flood*) was on top of his roof. He waited for three hours (*in a boat/on his roof*), and then two young men (*came in a boat/swam to him*) and (*brought him some money/took him to higher ground*). But he was sorry, because he did not (*have any money for them/want to go*).

Exercise 3

> Use *much* or *many* in questions (e.g. "Are there many people here?" "Is there much water here?") and in negative statements (e.g. "There aren't many people here." "There isn't much water here.").
>
> Use *a lot (of)* in affirmative statements (e.g. "There are a lot (of people) here." "There is a lot (of water) here.").
>
> Use *much* for a thing which we can't count (e.g. *water*), and *many* for more than one person, animal or thing that we can count (e.g. *women, cats, houses*).
>
> Use *a lot (of)* both for things that we can't count, and for persons, animals and things that we can count.
>
> Use *a lot of* when a noun follows (e.g. "There are a lot of people here."), and *a lot* (without *of*) when a noun does not follow (e.g. "And there are a lot here, too.").

Put *a lot, a lot of, many* or *much* in the empty places:

1 The old man did not have . . . money, and the Red Cross did not send . . . men.

2 "Do you have . . . rain here?" "Yes, we have . . . ." "Oh? We don't have . . . ."

3 There was . . . rain last night.

4 "Do . . . people live here?" "No, not . . . ."

5 There were . . . people in the flood, and . . . on the higher ground.

11

Mrs Walker has one son. His name is Harry. When he was four years old, he had a child's bicycle. It was red and white, and it had small wheels at its sides, so it always stayed up.

Then Harry did not have a bicycle for a long time. Now he is twelve years old, and he wants a bicycle.

Mrs Walker goes to work by car every day, and she takes Harry with her to his school, and brings him back when he finishes. His school is on one side of the town, and Mrs Walker's office is on the other side.

"A lot of my friends have bicycles, and they ride to school on them," Harry said to his mother one day. "Their mothers don't need to take them to school and bring them home again."

But his mother said to him, "Wait, Harry. Your father and I are going to buy you a nice bicycle soon."

Then yesterday Mrs Walker stopped her car at a red light and looked at Harry. "Harry," she said to him, "your father and I are going to give you a bicycle next month, but first I'm going to ask you some questions. Now, look at those traffic lights. Do you know their meaning?"

"Oh, yes, I do!" Harry answered happily. "Red is 'Stop', green is 'Go', and yellow is 'Go very quickly.' "

33

Exercise 1

Look at these questions. Find the right answers. Then write the questions and the answers:

1 Is Harry a boy, or a man?
   a) He is a boy.   b) He is a man.

2 Has his mother got a car?
   a) No, she has not.   b) Yes, she has.

3 Has she got a job?
   a) No, she has not.   b) Yes, she has.

4 Is Harry's school near her office?
   a) No, it is not.   b) Yes, it is.

5 Has Harry got a bicycle now?
   a) No, he has not.   b) Yes, he has.

6 What does he want?
   a) A bicycle.   b) A car.

7 What do a lot of his friends do?
   a) They drive to school in their cars.   b) They ride to school on their bicycles.

8 Where did Mrs Walker stop her car yesterday?
   a) At a bicycle shop.   b) At some traffic lights.

9 What did she ask Harry then?
   a) The meaning of her questions.   b) The meaning of the traffic lights.

10 Did Harry know the right meaning of the yellow light?
   a) No, he did not.   b) Yes, he did.

Exercise 2

Write this story. Choose the right words each time:

Mrs Walker is Harry's (*daughter/mother*). First Harry had (*a small bicycle/some small wheels*), but then he did not have (*any/one*). Now he goes to his (*office/school*) in (*his/his mother's*) car every day, but he wants to go by (*bicycle/bus*). A lot of other

34

boys have (*bicycles/cars*), so their mothers (*do not take/take*) them to school. Harry's mother (*did not need/needed*) to take Harry to school, because he (*did not have/had*) a bicycle, but then she wanted to buy one for (*him/his father*). But first (*he/she*) asked (*her/him*) a question about traffic lights, and (*her/his*) answers were (*all/not all*) right, because the meaning of yellow (*is/is not*) 'Go very quickly'.

Exercise 3

> We use *he/him/his* when we are writing about a man or a boy, *she/her* when we are writing about a woman or a girl, and *it/its* when we are writing about an animal or a thing. We use *they/them/their* when we are writing about more than one person, animal or thing.
>
> We use *he/she/it/they* for the subject, *him/her/it/them* for the object, and *his/her/its/their* to show possession.

Put *he*, *him*, *his*, *it*, *its*, *she*, *her*, *they*, *them* or *their* in the empty places:

1 This is Mrs Walker. . . . is in . . . car. . . . is blue. . . . wheels are dirty.

2 Mrs Walker has one son. . . . name is Harry. . . . goes to school. . . . mother takes him there. Harry is talking to . . . .

3 These are traffic lights. . . . are red now. Harry is looking at . . . . There are a lot of cars here. . . . drivers are waiting.

12

Harold Scott sold cheap shoes. He had a small lorry, and he bought the shoes from the factory and took them from one house to another and tried to sell them to people.

He sold a lot of his shoes in small villages, because there were not many shops there, and people did not want to go to the town and buy their shoes there.

One day Harold drove along the street of a village and stopped in front of one of the houses. There was a small boy beside the door. Harold opened the window of his lorry and called to the boy, "Hello. Is your mother at home?"

The boy looked at him. Then he answered, "Yes, she is."

"That's good," Harold said, and he smiled. He got out of his lorry, took some shoes from the back and went to the door of the house. He knocked at the door and then he waited, but the door did not open.

After a minute, Harold knocked at the door again and waited for two minutes, but again the door did not open.

Then Harold looked at the small boy and said in an angry voice, "Your mother is *not* at home."

"She *is*," the small boy answered.

"Then why hasn't she opened the door?" Harold asked.

"Because this isn't my house," the small boy answered.

Exercise 1

Look at these questions. Find the right answers. Then write the questions and the answers:

1 What did Harold do with his lorry?
a) He carried his shoes in it.   b) He took things from houses in it.

2 Who bought a lot of his shoes?
a) People in shops.   b) People in small villages.
c) People in the town.

3 What did Harold see in front of one house in a village?
a) A lorry.   b) A small boy.

4 What did Harold do to the boy?
a) He called to him.   b) He took him in his lorry.

5 Why did Harold take some shoes out of his lorry then?
a) Because he wanted to sell them to the boy.   b) Because he wanted to sell them to the boy's mother.

6 Did the boy's mother open the door?
a) No, she did not.   b) Yes, she did.

7 What did Harold do then?
a) He knocked again.   b) He opened the door.

8 Was he happy then?
a) No, he was not.   b) Yes, he was.

9 Was the boy's mother in the house?
a) No, she was not.   b) Yes, she was.

10 Why?
a) Because she was at the shops.   b) Because it was not her house.

Exercise 2

Write this story. Choose the right words each time:

Harold Scott (*did not make shoes, but he/made shoes in a factory and*) brought them to people's houses in a lorry. People in (*the town/villages*) bought a lot of his shoes, because (*there were not many shops/they did not want to buy shoes*) there. One day Harold was in (*his lorry/one of the houses*) in a village. He saw a small boy near a (*door/window*). He opened (*his window/it*) and (*smiled at/spoke to*) the boy. Harold was (*happy/sad*) because the boy's mother was (*at home/out*). He wanted to sell her (*his lorry/some of his shoes*). He knocked at the (*back/door*) of the house, (*and/but*) the boy's mother (*did not open/opened*) it. Harold (*looked at/spoke to*) the boy angrily then, but the boy was (*right/wrong*): his mother (*was/was not*) at home, but her home (*was/was not*) that house.

Exercise 3

> For *a*, *an* and *some*, see Unit 1. We use *the* instead of *a*, *an* or *some* when we refer back to something or someone that we have already mentioned. When we read, "This is a pen, and that is a pencil. The pen is black, and the pencil is red.", we know in the second sentence which pen and pencil the person is writing about — the ones he has written about in the first sentence.

Put *a*, *an*, *some* or *the* in each empty place:

Harold had . . . lorry. . . . lorry was quite small. Last Monday he took . . . money out of his bank and bought . . . shoes with it. He took . . . shoes to . . . village. He sold them in . . . village in . . . hour, and got a lot of money. Then he bought . . . more shoes with . . . money, and he bought . . . food for his family too. He has . . . wife and . . . eleven-year-old daughter.

13

Dick lived in England. In January he said to his wife, "I'm going to fly to New York next week, because I've got some work there."

"Where are you going to stay there?" his wife asked.

"I don't know yet," Dick answered.

"Please send me your address from there in a telegram," his wife said.

"All right," Dick answered.

He flew to New York on January 31st and found a nice hotel in the centre of the city. He put his things in his room and then he sent his wife a telegram. He put the address of his hotel in it.

In the evening he did not have any work, so he went to a cinema. He came out at nine o'clock and said, "Now I'm going to go back to my hotel and have a nice dinner."

He found a taxi, and the driver said, "Where do you want to go?" But Dick did not remember the name and address of his hotel.

"Which hotel are my things in?" he said. "And what am I going to do tonight?" But the driver of the taxi did not know, so Dick got out and went into a telegraph office. There he sent his wife another telegram, and in it he wrote, "Please send me my address at this telegraph office."

Exercise 1

Look at these questions. Find the right answers. Then write the questions and the answers:

1 Why did Dick fly to New York?
   a) Because his home was there.   b) Because he had work there.

2 Why did his wife want a telegram from him?
   a) Because he did not know his address yet.   b) Because she wanted to go to New York too.

3 Where did Dick stay in New York?
   a) With a friend in the centre of the city.   b) In a hotel.

4 Did he remember to send his wife a telegram?
   a) No, he did not.   b) Yes, he did.

5 Did he work that evening?
   a) Yes, in a cinema.   b) No, he did not.

6 Where did he want to go at nine o'clock?
   a) To a cinema.   b) To his hotel.

7 Did he want to walk to it?
   a) No, he wanted to go in a taxi.   b) Yes, he did.

8 What did the driver of the taxi want to know?
   a) The name and address of a telegraph office.   b) The name and address of Dick's hotel.

9 Did Dick tell him?
   a) No, he did not.   b) Yes, he did.

10 Who sent him the name and address of his hotel?
   a) A telegraph office.   b) His wife.

Exercise 2

Write this story. Choose the right words each time:

Dick's home was in (*England/New York*). He went (*there/to New York*) in January. He (*did not know/knew*) his address there, and his wife (*asked for it/knew it as well*). Dick went to New York in a (*plane/ship*) and found (*a room in/the address of*) a hotel. Then he sent (*his things/the address*) to his wife. He went to (*a cinema/his work*) in the evening, and then he wanted to have dinner (*and then go to/in*) his hotel. He got into a taxi, (*and told the driver/but he forgot*) the name and address of his hotel. The driver did not (*help him/answer*), so Dick got (*into another taxi/out*). He sent his wife a telegram from (*a telegraph office/his hotel*), and asked her for (*her/his*) address.

Exercise 3

> Use *come/bring* when the movement is towards you, and *go/take* when it is not (e.g. If I am in France, I can say, "I'm going to England tomorrow, and I'm coming back to France on Monday.").

Put *bringing, coming, going* or *taking* in the empty places:

1 Dick is . . . up to his room now.

2 Dick is . . . down again now.

3 A man is . . . Dick some food now.

4 And now he is . . . his empty plates.

41

14

Miss Miller lived beside a church in a small street in a town. She did not have a car. On Friday she always walked to the bus stop, and then she went to the market and bought food for the next week. There were usually a lot of people in the bus, but Miss Miller always found a seat.

One of the houses at the corner of Miss Miller's street was empty for a long time, but then a family came and lived in it. There was a man and his wife and two children. The children went to school in the bus in the morning.

On Friday Miss Miller went to the house and visited the children's mother. She said to her, "Good morning. My name's Jane Miller, and I live beside the church in this street. I'm going to the market now. Do you need any food?"

"Good morning," the woman said to her visitor, "you're very kind. My name's Mary Adams. Yes, I need food for my lunch today and for our supper tonight. And I need some fish for the cat. I don't know the way to the market yet. Can I come with you?"

"Please do," Jane answered. Mary put her coat on, and the two women went out and walked along to the bus stop. They waited there, and Jane said to her new friend, "There's a bus at five minutes to ten. It's always full, but I get a seat."

"Oh? Is that easy?" Mary asked.

Jane smiled and answered, "Wait and you'll see."

The bus came, and the two women got in. It was full, but Jane said, "Perhaps those two very handsome men will give us their seats."

Six men stood up quickly, and both the women went and sat down in the nearest seats.

Exercise 1

Look at these questions. Find the right answers. Then write the questions and the answers:

1 Did Miss Miller go to the market in her car?
   a) No, she did not.   b) Yes, she did.
2 Why?
   a) Because she always walked there.
   b) Because she did not have a car.
3 Was the bus usually nearly empty, or nearly full?
   a) Nearly empty.   b) Nearly full.
4 Why did Jane Miller visit Mary Adams's house?
   a) Because she wanted to help her.   b) Because she wanted to get some food from her.
5 Did Mary need food?
   a) No, she did not.   b) Yes, she did.
6 Why didn't she go to the market earlier that day?
   a) Because she did not need any food.   b) Because she did not know the way.
7 Who went with her?
   a) Her cat did.   b) Jane did.
8 Where did they walk to?
   a) To the bus stop.   b) To the market.
9 Were there any empty seats in the bus?
   a) No, there were not.   b) Yes, there were a lot.   c) Yes, there were two.
10 Did Mary and Jane get seats?
   a) No, they did not.   b) Yes, they did.

Exercise 2

Write this story. Choose the right words each time:

Miss Miller always went to the (*bus stop/market*) in the bus. It was always full, (*and/but*) Miss Miller (*always/never*) had to stand in it. There (*weren't any/were four*) people in one house in Miss Miller's street, but then a family came there. Miss Miller visited the house (*after/before*) she went to the (*church/market*) on Friday. The name of the woman in the house was (*Jane Miller/Mary Adams*). She (*did not have/had*) children, (*and/but she had*) a cat.

She (*did not want/wanted*) to go to the market, so the two women went (*for a walk/to the bus stop*). They got into a bus. There (*were a lot of/weren't any*) empty seats, (*and/but*) Jane and Mary (*did not get any/got two*).

Exercise 3

> When the subject of one of the forms of the verb *to be* is indefinite (i.e. when it has *a*, *an* or *some*, and not *the*), we usually have this order: *There is/are* + *a/an/some* + subject + adverb (phrase) (e.g. "There is a bus at 12 o'clock." "There are some flowers in Mary's garden.").
>
> But we use *he/she/it is* when we are referring to a person, animal or thing which has recently been mentioned (e.g. "The bus is coming. It is late."); and we use *they are* when we are referring to more than one person, animal or thing when they have recently been mentioned (e.g. "Jane has flowers in her garden. They are pretty.").

Put *he is*, *she is*, *it is*, *there is*, *there are* or *they are* in the empty places:

1 . . . a bus at ten o'clock. . . . always full.

2 . . . a lot of people in the bus. . . . young.

3 . . . a man in the front seat. . . . handsome.

4 . . . a little girl in the next seat. . . . very pretty.